17 Ways to grow your business at ZERO cost!

By Darren Hignett

Published: 28 October 2020.

Updated 5 January 2021

INTRODUCTION

Welcome to **17 ways to grow your business at zero cost!** This book has been designed to give you simple and easy to follow ways to find new customers and grow your business - without having to spend a fortune or hire technical or professional expertise.

By following the smart techniques in this book, you won't need to fork out hundreds or thousands of pounds, dollars or Euros on advertising spend to reach your target audience. Each tactic is easy to implement and doesn't require technical skills or knowledge in areas such as website design, coding, advanced marketing techniques (such as SEO) or even rocket science!

If your business is struggling to grow, or if you are growing but want to grow even faster, then use the advice in this book straight away. This book is designed to cover various types of businesses, whether you are a fitness trainer, accountant, fashion retailer or restaurant owner. This book is for you.

Once you have read this book, if you would like to take your growth to the next stage then feel free to contact me on darren@darrenhignett.com for a free chat to see how we can work together.

I hope you find this book of high value. Enjoy!

IS THERE REALLY ZERO COST INVOLVED?

Other than the very affordable price of buying this book, **you don't have to spend anything to implement these proven tactics**. There are, however, a couple of things you might want to consider:

First, although there is no cost involved implementing these tactics, there is still the consideration of how much time is needed to implement them. I have chosen tactics that get you the best results, not just because they cost nothing, but also because they are relatively quick and easy to implement and you should achieve great results in very little time. Having said that, some tactics take more time and effort than others, and you will need to decide which tactics to focus on most.

As you read through this book, make notes on what actions you can take that are specific to your business. I strongly recommend writing down one action at the end of each chapter, related to that tactic, that you can implement to get results. You don't have to read through the entire book before you get started. You might, for example, want to read the first 3 or 4 tactics and implement them into your business before you move onto the next 3 or 4 tactics in the book.

Another point to consider is that while these tactics might not cost anything to implement, you might want to increase their effectiveness by investing in resources and tools so that you can progress quicker. Facebook Ads and other advertising platforms can quickly help you reach more people at a relatively low cost while outsourcing some of the activities in this book to another staff member or an outsourcing agency will free up your time to focus on the tactics that get you better results.

If you do decide to invest money into these tactics, make sure to set a budget that you stick to and review your ROI (or return on investment). Spending 100 pounds or dollars on an Ads campaign means that you MUST return at least 101 pounds or dollars in profit! – not sales. If you compare your spend to the sales you get back then it could be that you are losing money on the campaign.

1. TAP INTO OTHER PEOPLE'S AUDIENCES

Marketing experts today will tell you how you should create a lead generation process that includes a special offer on your website and an email marketing campaign to sell your brand, products and services to your audience.

This is a great way to build a business long-term, but there are two issues.

Firstly, it takes time to build a list that includes hundreds of potential customers and by the time that you have built up your list, many of the subscribers (or their details) might be out of date as employees have changed jobs, companies you are targeting might have gone out of business or potential customers have either decided not to buy or have bought elsewhere.

A second issue is that, to make it really work, you need to invest in targeted ads that can cost a lot of money over time. Once you have built up your target audience, it's important to keep it refreshed and up to date, and this requires spending more again on ads.

There is, however, a quicker way to reach a larger audience, and it's by accessing someone else's audience.

Imagine, instead of spending months building up an email list to sell to, you feature on someone else's podcast or at their event. They might already have hundreds of followers listening to their podcasts or at their event.

> "Featuring in podcasts, magazines, interviews, and at events for just 10-15 key partners you have identified over a 12-month period can be 10 or 15 times more effective"

By tapping into their audience, you can quickly reach a large number of potential customers and demonstrate your expertise and knowledge to them.

To benefit from someone else's audience, the first step is to write down a list of potential key partners who have a similar target audience to you. Then create wording to send to them via email or another form of communication offering to feature at their event or podcast.

The opportunity grows exponentially when you reach out to multiple audiences. Featuring in podcasts, magazine articles, interviews and at events for just 10-15 key partners that you have identified over a 12-month period can be 10 or 15 times more effective than building a lead generation process.

To be clear – a lead generation process is still a great way to grow a business and I fully encourage you set this up but, tapping into another person's audience is a clever way to get more customers, quicker… and at zero cost.

Suggested Action: Write down a list of 5-6 key partners that you can contact. Make sure they meet the criteria of having a large target audience that you want to sell to. Once you have done this, establish contact with them and offer to support them with their podcast or other media channel that they use. Here's an example scenario:

Janice provides individual coaching on healthy eating and sells online courses and recipes for healthy eating.

She identifies a local gym that provides a weekly newsletter to its 200 members, a personal fitness trainer that provides a podcast to their 300 followers and a mindfulness coach that has several corporate clients that she delivers mindfulness tips (including mindful eating) to their employees (200 in total).

Janice contacts all 3 potential key partners and makes an offer to each of them.

For the gym, she might offer to give away her eBook if it features in their newsletter. For the fitness trainer, she might offer her time to feature on the podcast with some eating tips and, for the mindfulness coach, she might offer her eBook to their customers so that the coach can add value to her corporate clients.

If all 3 potential partners take up Janice's' offer then she will have reached a potential of 700 potential customers and, it gets better... because the gym, instructor or coach is effectively recommending Janice, potential customers are more likely to trust Janice, resulting in a higher take up of her products.

2. TRACK AND CONTINUE TO PROSPECT

80% of purchases are made after 5-12 contact points

48% of salespeople never follow up after the FIRST touchpoint

while only 10% of salespeople will make more than 3 'contacts'[1]

As you can see from the above figures, many businesses are missing out on sales!

The more contact you establish with a potential customer, the more likely they are to purchase from you – yet sales teams regularly give up after the first attempt, in pursuit of someone else who they hope will buy after the first conversation.

"a quick chase up email can be a very easy way of generating sales quickly"

The reason it takes so many contact points is that trust needs to be built up with the potential customer. The more interactions they have with you, the more likely they are to buy. With low value items, the number of contact points is typically lower but with high-priced items, such as buying a car, or the more personal the service, such as hiring an accountant or fitness trainer, then more touch points ae needed.

Touchpoints can range from face-to-face chats, interacting with potential clients over social media or even offering a free trial or eBook.

---

[1] Information from https://jmjdirect.wordpress.com/2010/01/14/how-many-contacts-does-is-take-to-make-a-sale-follow-up-is-the-key/ Although this data is quite old, similar more recent articles quote similar figures.

The more variation you offer in terms of touchpoints, the more likely you are to convert potential customers. If a customer says no to your services over the phone then they might be more likely to buy from you if you switch the conversation and build trust on other channels such as social media or email marketing rather than just using the phone.

When prospecting, design a process to follow up on enquiries. A CRM or Customer Relationship Management app is recommended so that you can track who you have contacted, when and why. You can also set reminders to follow up so that you don't forget.

If you don't use a CRM or don't have a spreadsheet of potential customers who have been in contact but not bought from you - then now is the time to start.

A CRM app is a great tool for tracking prospects and increasing the chances of converting enquiries into sales. If you don't want to start using a CRM app just yet then simply open a spreadsheet and start entering anyone who has contacted you in the last few months or years.

Add a column with the current status and another column with the next steps to take. For example, you might have received an enquiry 3 months ago from someone who didn't purchase. If you add them to the spreadsheet along with the action to drop them a quick email asking if they are still interested, then there is a chance that they will buy from you.

Sometimes the act of a quick chase up email can be a very easy way of generating sales quickly.

Suggested Action: A well-oiled process that's automated is best but, if you don't have a system set up, then start with some simple actions. Create a spreadsheet (or use a CRM) and add all potential prospects who you have interacted with in the last 6 months. For each potential prospect, add an action to re-establish contact. Here are some example scenarios:

John – called up a month ago asking about the prices you charge. You have his email address so send him an email asking if he has any further questions. Possibly offer him 10% off the prices that you originally sent as a one-off special offer.

Sally – downloaded your free eBook 3 months ago. You never followed up and don't have a sales lead generation process set up. Consider sending an email asking what she thought of the eBook and asking if you can be of any further assistance.

3. UPSELL/CROSS-SELL TO EXISTING CUSTOMERS

Do your customers know about all the products and services you offer?

You might be surprised by the reality to the above question. Quite often customers don't know about all the products and services you sell. They may have been with you for years and gotten used to the same great service but neither you or the customer has brought up the conversation of "what else do you offer?"

There are many ways you can communicate the different service you offer but having a catch-up call to discuss their requirements is a great way as you can spend time understanding their needs and how the different products or services you offer can help them. Alternatively, dropping them a quick email is a great way to upsell and to cross-sell.

For example, a customer who is on your standard package might want to upgrade to your premium service that's 20% higher priced. Alternatively, they might want to buy extras such as accessories or service plans and, in many situations, they might not know about the other products or services that you offer, even though they have been your customer for a long time!

If you don't have a premium plan, service plans or accessories to offer, then now might be the time to create upsell and cross-sell products.

You can also create a product/client matrix to identify which customers are buying which products or services from you. This will help you to identify gaps and opportunities to sell more to existing customers. Below is an example of a product/client matrix in action.

If you would like a free product/client matrix that you can use for your business, email me at darren@darrenhignett.com.

Product/client matrix example

Imagine that you have 3 products and 4 customers. We will label the customers as Customer 1, Customer 2 and so on, and the different products as Product A, Product B etc.

When filling in the product/client matrix, customers are added in the first column while the products are added in the first row. When doing this for your business, I suggest adding the customers names or the name of their business. Don't label them as 'Customer 1' or 'Customer 2'. I'm only doing it this way as it's an example. The same applies for products. Use the name of the product or service that you offer.

You might sell bundles of goods and services. I recommend including bundles and package offers as products as well.

	Product A	Product B	Product C
Customer 1			
Customer 2			
Customer 3			
Customer 4			

We can then fill in the matrix either by taking a product focus or a customer focus. For example, which customers use Product A (product focus) or which products does Customer A buy (customer focus)?

There is no right or wrong approach, but I recommend taking a customer focus approach so that you can dig deeper into understanding the situation and the needs of each individual customer. This will help you to serve them better – and to generate more sales from them in the long-term.

We will now fill in the table using the customer focus approach...

Customer 1 either buys regularly or has bought products A and B from you, Customer 2 buys product C only, Customer 3 buys products A and C while Customer 4 buys products B and C.

The matrix would look like this:

	Product A	Product B	Product C
Customer 1	X	X	
Customer 2			X
Customer 3	X		X
Customer 4		X	X

Based on the above, you can then contact Customer 1 about Product C and Customer 2 about products A & B to let them know about the products and how they can benefit from buying them.

You might also run a limited time campaign for a specific product, say Product B, and tailor your message to Customer 2 and Customer 3.

Finally, make sure to update the matrix regularly. This is important as you acquire new customers and having a product/client matrix pinned to your office wall also serves as a reminder to talk about the different products you have when talking to clients.

Suggested Action: Create your own product/client matrix and work through contacting each client individually to make sure they are aware of the different products or services you offer and their benefits.

4. INCREASE THE PURCHASE FREQUENCY OF EXISTING CUSTOMERS

Servicing existing customers is proven to be lower cost in time and marketing spend than finding new customers, and another way to generate more revenue is to increase how frequently someone buys from you.

> *"It costs 5x more to attract a new customer than it does to retain an existing customer"*

Creating a loyalty scheme (no matter how simple it is) is a great example of how you can encourage people to visit your restaurant, cafe, or hotel more often. Loyalty marketing can also be used to reward customers who buy from a range of other businesses as well, whether it's car and boat hire, a retail shop or providing training. Here are some quick and simple ways to encourage repeat purchases:

- Buy 12 'entry tickets' for the price of 10
- 10% off your second and/or 5th order
- A stamp card with a FREE coffee or drink after 10 purchases (stamps)
- A quick email to customers who purchased 6 months ago, to let them know about a new product or new features you have launched
- A quick email to customers who have not purchased for 6 months, offering a discount on their next order as a 'welcome back' offer

While some of the above don't cost anything in terms of marketing spend, giving away a free coffee or 10% on future orders has a cost implication which should be weighed up against the extra revenues. If, for example, you know that most customers only purchase once, then offering a discount on a second order might dramatically increase repeat orders. That could be a lot more revenue as a result!

5. BUILD KEY ALLIANCES & PARTNERS

Working closely with related businesses is a great way to grow your business. Imagine you provide web design or PA services. If you work with a business coach, then they can add value to their customers by suggesting that they delegate admin work to you or that they grow their business with a more effective website.

By working together with key partners, you can both reduce the amount of time, money and effort put into finding new customers as you can leverage each other's contacts and relationships.

> "By working together with key partners, you can both reduce the amount of time, money and effort put into finding new customers"

It also makes the sales conversion much easier and the conversion rate from prospect to buyer much higher because prospects are being recommended. If your key partner recommends your services, then the power of being recommended will provide confidence to the prospect that you are a reliable and trustworthy source to buy from.

An electrician can work closely with a decorator, plumber or conservatory builder. A bookkeeper can work with an accountant to help clients stay on top of finances. A nutritionist can work with a personal fitness trainer... and so on.

If you haven't identified who you can partner up with to help each other's business, then spend 20 minutes right now. Write down a list of people you believe would be good to work with and start building the relationship with them.

6. JOIN VIRTUAL NETWORKING EVENTS

With the arrival of COVID, there has been a massive growth in online networking events and while the traditional ways of networking face to face over breakfast or in the evenings are a great way to build relationships, they cost money and take up time. Enter… virtual networking events.

Some virtual networking events cost money but there are plenty currently that are free, and many that offer a free trial or first visit for free. Virtual networking events take up less time as you don't have to travel and there generally seems to be more focus than when meeting face to face (many online events are just an hour long compared to the 2+ hours of some face-to-face meetings).

Using Google search, make a list of online events that are likely to have your target audience attending, and book yourself into them. If you find too many events then make sure to note them down anyway, including their website address. You can then prioritise the list and manage your time better. You might find that one event is much more effective than others and therefore you prefer to visit it again instead of others.

It's important when attending the event that you have clarity on your key message (see 'Clarify your message' further on in this book) and that you have a special offer. When presenting your business, it's better to say 'I help businesses make more profit with my accounting support and am offering a free initial chat (or profit-improvement session?)' rather than just 'I'm an accountant' (sigh, look down at shoes and avoid eye contact…).

7. CREATE A REFERRAL OFFER AND PROMOTE IT

Want a month of support for free or an Amazon voucher? Don't we all? If you create a referral offer that someone can benefit from then they are more likely to promote your business for you.

This has two great benefits. Firstly, if you have, say, 10 people promoting your product, then you effectively have 10 salespeople working for you. Okay, they might not be working on your business full-time for you, but you get the idea.

The second benefit is about trust. Who would you trust more - someone who says, "buy from me, my product is great" or someone who says, "Have you tried the products from this business, they are great"? People are more likely to buy when they are sold to 'indirectly' through a recommendation.

> "Once you have created a referral offer, make sure to promote it properly"

Once you have created a referral offer, make sure to promote it properly. Include it in your emails when sending out invoices, promote it on social media, remind customers when you talk to them regularly on the phone and even include it in your email signature.

Suggested action: Create a referral offer and add the offer immediately to your email signature, invoices and quotes that you send out. This should take very little time to set up and can be very effective.

8. USE FACEBOOK GROUPS & TWITTER

Social media is a great way to find and engage with customers, but it's easy to spend too much time on activities that don't grow your business. In this section, I focus on 2 tactics that are proven to get results and that take very little time if done properly.

It's worth pointing out that many businesses post regularly on social media, hoping it will lead to lots of sales. There are many benefits to posting regularly on social media, including social proof and the ability to build long-term relationships but generating lots of sales is NOT one of the many benefits.

We won't go into why it doesn't work in detail here but, one of the main reasons it's ineffective in generating sales is that the number of potential new customers who see these posts are low. Today, only 5-10% of fans who have liked a Facebook business page will see their posts – and the amount of people who will take action is even lower.

The tactics below are much more effective and take up a lot less time than posting daily on various social media platforms.

Facebook Groups

There are lots of Facebook Groups with hundreds, if not thousands of people in them - and they get higher visibility on posts than a Facebook business page does organically. Imagine you are selling cleaning services in Hampshire and there is a Facebook community called 'Businesses in Hampshire' with 2,000 members. Simply posting an offer in this group will mean that up to 2,000 members could see your post in a very short period of time.

Facebook groups are free to use but make sure you follow the rules of individual groups and don't post too many promotional posts in the same group. If you manage it properly, you can reach a lot of people in various groups in a very short period of time.

Use Twitter search to find prospects

From time to time, I hear the argument that Twitter isn't for them or for their business. I understand this and I understand that Instagram, TikTok and a few other platforms are growing and becoming more popular. Twitter, however, continues to be a great place to find opportunities if you know what to do.

Imagine you sell engagement and wedding rings. Search 'on their engagement' and you will see a range of tweets saying 'Congrats to NAME and NAME on their engagement. Looking forward to the big day'. Now you have the names of two people who might want wedding rings!

A dentist might search for 'toothache', a web designer might search for 'need a new website' and a recruitment consultant might search for 'been made redundant' or 'need work'. These are only examples and you might not like the ones I have chosen but you get the idea.

It's recommended to create various keywords to search and to develop a plan around how you approach the prospects without coming across as too much of a stalker! For two people getting engaged, you might just want to congratulate them (and possibly offer them 20% off?). For a dentist, you might want to give some basic tips or wish them well.

9. CLARIFY YOUR MESSAGE

Making small changes to existing headlines and marketing materials can make a huge difference to your results!

Imagine looking through your local newsletter, looking for someone to clean your patio which is in urgent need of sorting out. You come across two different businesses advertising their services. Which of the two headlines below are you more likely to respond to?

Headline one: Johnsons Gardening Ltd

Headline two: We'll make your patio super clean, or your money back!

Headline two, right? How about in this instance?

Headline one: Landscape gardening done for you

Headline two: Professional, proven experts in patio cleaning

Again, you are more likely to go with headline two. When it comes to having the right messaging for your business, the headline is, without any doubt, THE most important area to get right. Just changing your headline from your brand name to explaining what you do, and the benefits, could easily lead to a 20-30% increase in sales.

When it comes to simple tactics that are free, it doesn't get much better and easier than changing your headline in marketing materials.

There are various elements to a headline that can get results. Power words, for example, are words that the human brain reacts to such as 'now', 'limited time', 'proven' and 'guaranteed'. Other elements include how clear your message is and how compelling the benefits are of what you offer.

Here are some quick tips for improving headlines:

- Avoid having, or just stating, your company name
- Focus on the benefits or the single greatest benefit
- Consider power words
- Be specific. The more specific you are, the more likely a customer wanting that service will contact you
- Test the headline by adding the following sentence at the end 'contact us today on xxx'. Then ask friends and colleagues if it makes sense and urges them to want to buy

Clarity on your messaging isn't just about headlines (although it is possibly the most important part of your marketing communication!). Potential customers need to understand what you do and why they should buy from you (in other words, the benefits!).

If your website and anything else that comes into contact with your customer doesn't have clear messaging, then you could be losing sales.

Readers of this book are entitled to a free Scientific Marketing Makeover which highlights where you can improve your messaging. You can claim your free 'makeover' by clicking here.

Suggested Action: Review all of your marketing messaging to see what minor changes you can make that will improve their effectiveness and if you need any help, take up my offer of a Scientific Marketing Makeover… it's free.

10. CREATE UNIQUENESS

Providing uniqueness in what you offer can be incredibly effective in growing your business!

Why should customers buy from you? Sometimes it can be that they are familiar with you or your brand, or that they trust you more than your competitor. There are many reasons why someone might buy from you, but there are also many reasons why they might buy from your competitor.

One way to make your proposition more compelling is by providing something that's unique. If you are the only business that provides extra support and resources or a product feature that no one else offers, then it's much harder for a potential customer to say no to buying from you.

If you aren't clear on what you offer, or can offer, that's unique, then brainstorm and write down a list of potential ways that you can be unique. This could include one or more of the following:

- Out of hours support
- Bundled solutions
- An unrivalled guarantee
- Extra free resources or templates
- Faster delivery
- Local support
- Personal support
- A Facebook support group
- A patented design or feature

Sometimes being unique can be created from a range of elements which, when brought together create a proposition that nobody else offers. Apple™ has built its brand this way.

You might be able to find a product elsewhere that's cheaper or has more features or is backed up by better support but when you buy an Apple iPhone or iPad you are buying a brand that is a unique combination of style, reliability and features that's hard for any competitor to replicate.

The Apple brand and its uniqueness has been built up over the years and can't be replicated just by creating a device that beats Apple on one factor, such as feature set or reliability.

When it comes to coming up with how you can be unique, brainstorming or bouncing ideas off a colleague, marketing mentor or friend is a great way to generate ideas for how you can provide uniqueness to your customers.

The more unique your offering, the harder it is for your competition to copy you. It's also important to make sure that the way in which you are unique also adds value to your customers. Being the only business that wears purple clothes and paints your van or business car in purple might be unique, but it doesn't add value to your customer!

Coming up with something unique doesn't cost anything. What you offer that's unique might have a cost associated to it, but it's worth taking a different perspective on this.

If the extra support you provide, for example, brings in 30% more sales, but takes up little extra of your time, then it's worth offering.

Note: Most of the time, customers don't take advantage of extra support hours or features. If you offer extra back-up support to 100 customers, it's possible that only 5-10% (or 5-10 customers) will use the extra service.

One last point on being unique – make sure to include it in your messaging. I see many businesses who think they are unique for various reasons but when you look at their website, quotes they provide, and other materials, it's not mentioned!

Your potential customer needs to know that what you offer is unique. Don't leave them guessing!

Suggested Action: Work out what's unique about your brand or your products and services. If it's not compelling enough, consider working towards creating uniqueness by modifying what you offer and designing new services that offer that uniqueness.

11. FOCUS ON LOW HANGING FRUIT

… but have a sales process for each level of 'customer buying readiness'.

Potential customers can be at different levels of readiness to buy, as follows:

1. No intent: Unaware they need your service or of the benefits. They need to be 'educated'
2. General research: Not looking to buy. Just want to understand the product and benefits
3. Buying research: Looking to buy but researching the options
4. Interested: More than 50% likely to buy from you but asking for more information
5. Ready to buy: They want what you offer and are enquiring how to place an order

Potential customers at level 1 require a lot of work and effort. They might really need your service but aren't aware that they do.

Take a nutritionist or health coach offering ways to get healthier. A potential customer might not think that they need support or help. They might believe that they are fine as they are, until they face a health scare, or they wake up one day and read an article by the nutritionist which talks about the benefits of being healthier.

Customers at level 1 need to be educated as to what you offer and the benefits. They need you to provide them with valuable blog posts, YouTube videos and a lead generation process that sends them emails with top tips and helpful advice so that they can learn about your products and what they do for them.

Potential customers at level 2, however, require less effort to drive them to a sale, while those at level 3, 4 and 5 typically require, respectively, less time and money convincing them to buy. It might, therefore, make sense to focus on level 5 customers, but the downside here is that there are most likely to be only a small number of customers at this level for your business.

When it comes to focusing on the 'low hanging fruit' (the potential sales that are quick and easy to win without spending too much money on sales and marketing efforts), the best area to concentrate on is customers at level 3 and 4. They are already looking for potential solutions and just need you to show them why they should buy from you.

To focus on potential customers at levels 3 and 4, here are some actions to take:

- Create templated wording for typical questions that you get via email. Make sure it includes a call to action and if possible, an offer
- Define a process for chasing up if someone doesn't buy after making an enquiry. This can be a simple email that says 'hey, did that answer your question and is there anything else we can help with?'. Remember – more contact touch points = higher chances of customers buying
- Review past enquiries and customers and try to re-establish contact where relevant. Previous customers understand the benefits of what you offer and are more likely to come back and buy from you.

As well as addressing the quick wins, make sure you have a sales process for each level. This is key to long-term success and, while it doesn't need to be urgently done, it's still something that should be implemented.

12. REVERSE THE RISK FOR THE CUSTOMER

The more a product costs and the bigger the commitment, the more cautious a potential customer is. If you are selling cans of cola on a busy street on a hot day, then people passing by are likely to make what's called an 'impulse purchase'. The decision process is very short before the purchase is made.

Buying a car, a house or furniture for the lounge, on the other hand, requires a lot more thought – not just over what colour or design, but also on questions such as 'do I trust who I am buying from?' and 'will I get a better service if I buy from someone else?'. If there is any doubt, the customer is likely to disappear off to buy elsewhere quicker than a greyhound chasing a rabbit. But, how to address this?

The answer is easy. Simply reverse the risk for the customer. There are many ways you can do this, such as by building up testimonials and reviews of your service or offering best-in-class after sales support but the most effective way is with an irresistible guarantee.

An irresistible guarantee is one which guarantees that the customer will be happy, or they get their money back. It's a guarantee that in some way, punishes you and your business if you don't deliver. This might sound harsh but by reversing the risk and taking it away from the customer, it becomes very hard for them to say no.

When Domino's Pizza went into business, they created a simple guarantee – piping hot pizza in 30 minutes or your money back. They grew their business from a single outlet to becoming a worldwide brand based on a guarantee that customers loved.

Were they worried that it might cost them millions of dollars or pounds in free pizzas? Probably. But it helped them to focus on delivering great customer service. They offered something unique at the time and provided a guarantee that took away the risk of buying from them.

There is always a risk for a business that a guarantee might backfire and cost money, but, providing the business delivers to the standard that it should, then there should be very low or zero cost to the business. And the business will benefit with a much higher growth in sales and higher conversion rates.

If your business doesn't offer a guarantee that provides risk reversal for the customer then take an action now to create one. It should be easy to implement and will really help to grow your business.

13. FIND, FOLLOW AND ENGAGE ON LINKEDIN

LinkedIn is a great way to reach out to and build trust with new and existing customers!

LinkedIn has become a great tool for finding potential customers but there are two things that not many people realise. Firstly, that it's possible to follow potential contacts rather than connect with them (which requires them to accept your invitation). Secondly, that you can find contacts by using Google!

Imagine that your target audience is HR Managers, and you want to find the HR manager of a company called Leaf Investments (a totally fictional name in case you try to search for it).

Head over to Google and search using the format: **job role + Company name + LinkedIn** which in the above example would be 'HR Manager Leaf Investments LinkedIn'.

Searching on Google doesn't always yield the results you want, but from my personal experience, it brings back good results more than 80% of the time. Once you have found the right contact, visit them on LinkedIn and interact with them. Here are the steps to take:

1. Find the contact on Google
2. Click on the Google search result to see their profile
3. Click on 'Follow' rather than invite them to connect
4. View their posts and like a post you genuinely like
5. Over the next few weeks, check back to see what they have posted and like or comment where possible
6. Once you feel it's the right time, invite them to connect and send them a personal message to take the relationship to the next level

The aim of the above process is to build trust with a potential client so that they are open to talking to you. Many people on LinkedIn go straight for the jugular by inviting someone who doesn't know them to connect. They then try to sell them something straight away. This is a great way to annoy or alienate a potential customer.

If you follow the above approach and take a measured approach to point 5 (i.e. don't like and comment on every post they do in one go!) then the potential customer is more likely to accept your LinkedIn request and listen to what you have to say.

The above process might be more relevant if your business is selling B2B (Business to Business) but it can also apply with B2C (or Business to Consumer) businesses as well.

A home cleaning business, for example, might connect with professionals who don't have the time to maintain their homes at a high level, but they do have the money to hire a cleaner.

Take an action to write down a list of roles and companies that you would like to target. Then set an action to search for 5-10 contacts a day to get you started. Over a 5-day week, this can quickly add up to following 50 potential new customers a week (or 200 a month!).

14. USE GOALS TO STAY FOCUSED

"Figuring out what you are supposed to produce, and learning the priorities in the creation, quality, and frequency of that output, is one of the greatest breakthroughs you can have in your career"

~ Brendon Burchard, High Performance Habits

This might seem a bit different to the previous tactics so far, but it's possibly the most important one. Evidence shows that having goals leads to better results - and staying focused on goals increases the chances of success even more!

When it comes to running your own business, it's easy to get distracted with emails and other activities. It's easy to procrastinate and lose focus, but if you have clear goals that are written down – and that are at the front of your mind throughout the day – then you will grow your business.

In my free eBook 'How to set goals that get results', I talk about the **Stranger in the street test** that goes like this:

Imagine you are stopped by a stranger in the street who asks you what your goals are. You probably wouldn't want to share this with a stranger but bear with me… would you be able to tell them off the top of your head what your personal and business goals are?

If not, then it's worth revisiting your goals to ensure you have the clarity you need. At any point throughout your day, you should know what your goals are. This will help you on a conscious as well as a subconscious level to make sure that what you do on a daily, weekly and monthly basis is based on achieving your goals.

The simple fact is that if you set goals based around sales targets and focus on them daily, then you are more likely to do activities that get results. If you need help setting goals properly then I can help.

Alternatively, if you have never set goals before then create a single goal that's focused on achieving a sales target within a short timeframe and then write down the 4 or 5 activities that will help to grow your business. This is a great way to get started.

15. SELL OTHER BRANDS PRODUCTS

Every business has apps, tools and other products that they might recommend to customers. An accountant might tell customers what the best accounting software is, well as the best apps for tracking expenses, time taken to deliver a service and so on.

A fitness instructor might advise on healthy smoothies or fitness books and a guitar tutor might recommend music books and other accessories for tuning and playing a guitar.

Since setting up my business in 2011, I am surprised how many apps and platforms I have used on a regular basis, and I'm happy to admit that I recommend them to potential customers all the time, while also being able to make money from some of them.

This is done through affiliate links (when someone clicks on a link I provide; I earn a small fee if they sign up to use the product). This is nothing new. Even Amazon provides authors of audiobooks with a generous bonus if a customer signs up to a 30-day trial of Audible using a custom link which authors, including myself, can promote.

Another way to make money on products is to sell them directly, either by physically stocking or drop shipping them to a customer.

Drop shipping is a great way to make money while keeping costs and time down. When a customer orders from you, the goods are shipped directly from the original supplier to them. You don't need to stock the product or handle any inventory.

Whatever the approach, every business should aim to sell or make money on 5-10 complimentary products in addition to the products and services they offer themselves.

This will help to grow sales, either by providing the extra products as an upsell (therefore increasing the revenue earned per customer) or by reaching out to customers who might not usually be interested in your core products and services that you offer.

16. BUILD AN EMOTIONAL BANK ACCOUNT

In his book *7 habits of highly effective people*, Stephen Covey talks about the emotional bank account. The idea of doing something nice for someone is akin to making a deposit into someone's emotional bank account. When you need help or support from that person you are making a withdrawal from that same bank account, but if you haven't deposited anything then there's nothing to take… in other words, the other person is unlikely to want to help.

Business related examples include liking someone's posts because they have made an effort to like or comment on yours.

Similarly, if you pass on potential referrals to another business, they are more likely to refer back to you or help you out in some other, including possibly buying from you if what you offer fits their requirements.

Another, or similar, term for an emotional bank account is the law of reciprocity, which goes something like this: if someone does something for you or offers something for free to you then you are likely to want to return the favour (or reciprocate).

Whether it's an emotional bank account or the law of reciprocity, the way it can be applied in marketing and sales is the same. Help out or support someone and they are more likely to support you in return, whether that's endorsing you, referring you or even buying from you.

We have already talked about building trust with potential customers and one way to do this is to provide them with tips and support. Every time you do something nice for a customer, or provide them with value, then you are building trust and increasing their chances of buying from you.

Offering a free 30-day trial, for example, gives the customer a feeling that you have given something for free and they are more likely to reciprocate and make a purchase as a result.

Here are some ways you can use the law of reciprocity to encourage sales:

- A free trial of your software or online course
- A free consultation or coaching session
- Referring a potential client to them
- Sharing and commenting on their social media posts
- A free sample of your product
- Providing a genuine review of their services or recommend them to your customers
- A simple thank you for being a customer or key contact

If you have potential customers that you have interacted with, but they haven't yet bought from you then why not re-establish contact and offer them a free trial or sample?

Face to face (including remote) meetings are also more effective when making a deposit into the emotional bank account of your potential customer. This could include providing some great value advice during the meeting, sharing templates or freebies or offering a limited time trial at the end of the meeting.

Suggested action: Create a lead generation process where you offer value to a potential customer. This can be a free eBook, consultation or regular newsletter with tips and advice.

17. USE EMPATHY AND LISTENING TO SELL

Listening to your customers is a powerful way to delight them, and to grow your business. Understanding their issues and helping them helps make a sales pitch much easier, especially if, like most people, you don't like the idea of 'selling' to people.

Here's a process that will make a sales conversation more effective:

1. **Listen carefully** to their concerns and their situation. Don't provide advice at this stage, but do ask questions to understand further
2. **Repeat back a summary** of their issues or re-phrase it to show you have understood
3. If they have talked about possibly using your competitors' products, address that by agreeing on how that might be a solution for them, stating the pros and the cons
4. Based on what they have said, **highlight how your product or service might help**
5. If the customer is looking like they might buy**, make an offer**. Otherwise, repeat the above process to understand their concerns more.

Repeating back what someone says demonstrates to them that you were listening as well as re-enforcing it in your own mind, but you can take listening skills to the next level by re-phrasing what you have heard.

Re-phrasing means that you have to really listen carefully and think about what has been said. The extra brain power used to do this means that you are more likely to listen to and understand the situation of your client.

Be careful when repeating or re-phrasing not to do this too often as it can seem a bit robotic and almost as if you are joking around (anyone who has kids that repeat what you say will understand!).

Here is an example of how the conversation might go when selling an app that increases productivity for a customer:

Customer: The biggest problem I have is how long it takes to get the task done. If I hire someone then the costs will go up, but I don't have the time to do the work myself. I've looked at the ABC app (your competitors) which will allow me to get the tasks done quicker but it's quite expensive.

You: (still at level 1) How many hours does it take you to complete the task currently?

Customer: About 6 hours every day. And that doesn't include after sales support as well.

You: (now at level 2): So, you want to reduce the time it takes you to get the task done as it takes way too long. If you could reduce the 6-hours a day without incurring costs by hiring someone then that would be ideal?

Customer: Correct. I can't afford to increase costs for every transaction right now.

You: You could hire someone part time to reduce the workload slightly, while keeping your costs down. The ABC app might help improve productivity as well, but if it's too expensive then I guess it won't provide a huge amount of extra benefit.

Customer: Ok, understood.

You: The app we provide is lower cost and is proven to reduce the time it takes to perform tasks similar to what you do by 75%. In fact, we guarantee an increase in productivity, or you get your money back, so there are a few options.

Customer: Thanks, you seem to understand the challenges I face. I like the idea of the guarantee you provide.

You: (level 5) Thanks, if you want to give it a go, I'm happy to provide you with a 5-day trial and a free installation and orientation session to show you how the app works and to make sure you get the most out of it…

The above example is a much longer conversation than a direct approach of immediately selling the benefits of your product but, by spending the time to understand the needs and challenges of the customer, you can position your services better and build more trust with the customer.

Using empathy and understanding in any conversation with a potential customer is a highly effective tactic for growing your business.

SUMMARY

I hope you have enjoyed reading this book on how to grow your business (at zero cost!). Here's a summary of the 17 tactics or ways to grow your business without needing to spend money:

1. Tap into other people's audiences
2. Track and continue to prospect beyond the first point of contact
3. Upsell and cross-sell to existing customers to increase revenue per customer
4. Increase the purchase frequency of customers
5. Build key alliances and partners so you can mutually support each other
6. Join virtual networking events that are free
7. Create a referral offer and promote it
8. Use Facebook Groups and Twitter Search
9. Clarify your message to get better results
10. Create uniqueness
11. Focus on 'low hanging fruit'
12. Reverse the risk for the customer (with an irresistible guarantee)
13. Find, follow and engage on LinkedIn
14. Use goals to stay focused on sales
15. Sell other brands products
16. Build an emotional bank account with potential customers
17. Use empathy and listening to sell better

If you would like to learn more about more effective marketing, then you might be interested in the books listed below that I have also written.

If you have any questions or would like to contact me for support, then feel free to email me using darren@darrenhignett.com

Thanks for reading!

~ Darren

MORE READING...

The following books can be found on www.thinktwicemarketing.com/resources and might be of interest:

Psychology in Marketing and Sales

Blogging for business

How to create a perfect landing page

How to create a successful email marketing campaign

You might also be interested in the following blog posts:

3 marketing facts that will make you re-think what you are doing, including why just posting on social media doesn't get the best results:

https://www.thinktwicemarketing.com/blog/3-marketing-facts-that-will-make-you-re-think-what-you-are-doing

Warning: Is Your New Customer Coming Back? 4 Steps You Should Take Now, including some interesting facts on why customer loyalty is more cost effective than finding new customers:

https://www.forbes.com/sites/tjmccue/2013/02/04/warning-is-your-new-customer-coming-back-4-steps-you-should-take-now/?sh=568430e67feb

6 ways to create a call to action that generates leads, including what colors and wording to use:

https://www.thinktwicemarketing.com/blog/6-ways-to-make-a-call-to-action-that-generates-leads

www.ingramcontent.com/pod-product-compliance
Lightning Source LLC
Chambersburg PA
CBHW070336240526

45466CB00027B/2107